A journey of my Thoughts

Gaurav Anant Udavant

BlueRose ONE.com
Stories Matter

First Published in March 2022

ISBN: 978-93-93809-00-1

BLUEROSE PUBLISHERS

www.bluerosepublishers.com
info@bluerosepublishers.com
+91 8882 898 898

Cover Design:
Aveek

Typographic Design:
Rohit

Distributed by: BlueRose, Amazon, Flipkart

Foreword

Gaurav Anant Udavant is a qualified Automotive Digital Modeler. His passion for automobile design took him to Turin and Milan where he completed his Masters in Transportation Design. These are hardly the qualifications one would expect to see attached to someone who is now presenting a collection of poems.

What started as contributions of essays to the school magazine – The St. Xavier's Boys' Academy Chronicle, has metamorphosed into 'A Journey of My Thoughts.' Gaurav's poems are bound to resonate with many, especially the young at heart, as they deal with a range of subjects. After reading through some of his poems on topics like the quest for true love, romance, rejection, a longing for acceptance and the search for inner beauty, one can only be left amazed when told that these are purely imaginative and not part of any specific personal experience. And of course, there are poems on automobiles and everyday matters.

Do sit back and enjoy these poems, considering that this collection has been written over a period of barely a year and a half, one can look forward to another collection in the not too distant future.

Wishing this young poet, the very best as he channelizes his creativity into communicating in verse.

Savio D'Mello
Vice Principal – St. Xavier's Boys' Academy

Preface

I read a lot every day. I decided that it was time to put some of my thoughts into a book.

I have summed up about the notions I used to go through and wherever my mind travelled. Therefore, the name of the book. I first write my thoughts in sentences and then alter the words like that of a poem. These thoughts I used to enter into my mobile phone notes. I had mind blocks at times and at such times I used to let my mind wander. After I thought of something better, I used to come back to the poem. I have pursued writing poems as a hobby. I have written this collection of poems in a span of one and a half year.

Acknowledgements

At times I had day dreams and other times I used to simply stay awake in the middle of night thinking about something. It also used to be about my frustrations and encounters of people around me. But sometimes the reasons were good as well. I would like to thank my family, friends, teachers who taught me good languages skills and my colleagues at work who took the time to read or listen to my poems.

Contents

1
The Smart Woman

Like a lightning bolt, her questions strike my steady mind,
The aftermath of the encounter renders me stunned to unwind.

I do answer her, but find it difficult to get her approval,
Even though her words aren't so frugal.

Like when you start the engine,
The engine would run for long,
You start something interesting and she carries it along.

Her brain teasers have me falling into a maze of thoughts,
I don't mind it, for it is much better than having my brain gather moss.

Her inner beauty is what I seek;
From what I know,
There is barely anything about her I would critique.

2
Maniacs

They want to change the world but won't look at the mirror,
But challenge them, and they will shiver.

Give them the slightest of chance to criticise and they pounce on you,
Fools too criticise and ultimately bid their friendship adieu.

First change yourself and then the universe,
Jealousies and cruelties lead your character to sleep in the hearse.

Third grade are those who proudly show their anger,
Strutting along the aisle, behaving as if they have a cool swagger.

Let us see how long these bullies survive with ethics like this,
With violent speech and fault-finding, it is for time to tell us,
How long they will have their bliss.

3
Terrifying Obsession

Into her watery depths, she will pull you beneath,
Without saying a word, she will know all your secrets so deep.

I have gone too deep in her obsession now, it is difficult to come out,
It is no use now, it is too late to shout.

I am even short of breath now and almost blinded,
With her thoughts, I am all surrounded.

A smooth demeanour she has and may even steal your word,
Don't be surprised if she moves like the humming bird.

Yesterday she refused to make even the absolute of guesses,
In the very same way, the feelings that she represses.

4
Let Me Loose

Either strangle me, or leave me alone,
But don't keep me rooted with the seeds you have sown.

You like to play chase, and after a brief period,
You come back to embrace.

When I'm in the mood for fun,
You ignore me and you think you are done.

You like to lure me with your charisma,
Coming out of your secret world with a Syrma.

Stop! I have had enough!
Please! Cut out your fluff!

5
One Word

Her beauty? Astonishing!
When I look at her, my health is deteriorating.

When her message arrives? My heart is racing,
How do I reach my phone? Like Rahul Dravid in the slips, catching.

When she praises me? I am blushing,
What would I avoid doing with her? Arguing,
What's more within her? I have started discovering.

6
The Darkest

Black.
Have you ever seen this kind of black?
Looking at it, you hear the sound of silence without any knack.

You know if someone is near you,
And still are bothered why you can't see them in view.

You can see your past as well as imagine your future with it,
Then travel with your mind as far as it would permit.

It is deeper than the depths of the ocean,
And easily evokes extreme emotion.

It is clearly not neutral but yet it is the symbol of mystery,
You see it before you are born, and when you are history.

Close your eyes.
What do you see?
Black.

7
Black Magic Woman

When she steps into a room,
Using sharp sensitive sense she knows if there is happiness or gloom.

From her cold sharp bursts of breath,
And listening to your words, she can influence your health.

Mystery, lies and deceit surround her like black smoke,
With these, she intoxicates any innocent and bad bloke.

If you try to catch her tail,
As quick as a lizard, she disappears behind her veil.

8
Complexities

Is there a situation you are failing to comprehend?
Understanding the complexities that ascend?

Do what you can but don't pretend,
That you are okay with your suffering
And your self-esteem that keeps to descend.

Nip the problem in the bud
The next time it arises,
Or it could have a grave effect
To exponential sizes.

Do not drown in sorrow,
Deal with your fear like there is no tomorrow.

'Beyond your control' is what you say to yourself?
Persist to do what you should and the situation solves itself.

But hey, just know that not every thought that comes to mind is right,
Make an informed choice and know what is in sight.

9
Myself

Today I write about myself;
It is time to put everything else on the shelf.

Dreams are becoming real,
So much so, they seem surreal.

Passion so deep, it is like the blood running through my veins every day,
Today I received recognition for my past efforts, now it is time to make hay.

When they said no, I heard a yes,
Even those close to me, but now I have beaten this distress.

My thoughts were crushed a hundred times but I held on to only one support, my hope.
We somehow knew, that I still had scope.

100's and 100's of sleepless, crying nights and days I spent,
To catch that dream floating in mid-air and now I don't repent.

A single-minded mindset I followed and had no plan B,
I was given many an advice and options,
But only pursuing car design was all I could see.

Yet this is not where I want to be,
But I may be close to it, this is what I can see.

10
Race Against Time

Vroom! They went at speeds of
Distance per microsecond.
Fast enough that if you were watching them close,
You would be threatened.

Surpassing the post against several G forces,
With their internal organs being pushed back to the seat,
They were not afraid to be corpses.

Zooming past the corners,
Yerzhan and Arjun stole the show.
It was necessary to keep the endurance,
And not go slow.

While others got tired,
And lost concentration
They both were focused,
A lap ahead from the rest of the equation.

As the race neared its end,
The others started catching up.
But there occurred a crash,
That started with a tense rub.

Wham! Roll, boom, screech, whack, the cars slowed down,
But the rival pair wanted to complete the race,
And fight for the crown.

It was the last lap, and flooring the pedal,
Both went full throttle at the corners,
Straight around the corners,
And then swiftly accelerating for the honours.

Both finished the race with Yerzhan at the pole.
And no one to show for the 3rd position.

Out of the stands came all the ladies toward Yerzhan,
Like the effect of an atom bomb, almost like fiction.

The rival pair celebrated and went home,
With a huge trophy each in the end.
Thanks to Yerzhan and Arjun,
The audience was entertained to no end.

11
Her Eyes

Their sight and range extend till your heart.
She uses them to scan your motives,
Ask her whether they are real
And her answer tears you apart.

Hypnotic they are and make you dizzy,
Her penetrating and intense gaze will render you for a tizzy.

The more you look at her eyes, the more they suppress,
What lies beneath, you can never guess!

12
You

I have started to care for you a lot,
I hope not that in your life, I become a blot.

Those poems I wrote were all for you,
Now don't ask me why, because of the fondness that grew.

You taught me how to talk to a pretty girl,
I will forever be grateful to you, for making my mind unfurl.

You make my mind run like my car accelerating at full speed,
I hope now that in attaining your own dream house, you will succeed.

Do you know that life has always been unfair with me in matters of love?
I find it hard to believe, whether I will find my white dove.

But if you still have an open mind, and think I will be your good friend,
Please, because it is only you who can help me repair this feeling,
And come out of this in the end.

13
Red Beauty

Off she goes on the green signal, but painting the town red,
With her smooth curves and beautiful colour, her charm comes to a head.

With all the men staring at her,
She runs with a dither.

So shiny and sculpted is her body, that it gleams in the sun,
With all of the crowd watching now, there is no one she can shun.

You obviously think she must be Barbie,
But NO! She is a Ferrari.

14
Hope

When I look at her, I feel like I'm lying down on my back
And gazing at the stars, I am dreaming.

She won't believe me, as she always does not,
That she has inspired the poet in me.
She hides things I want to know the most about,
It does hurt, but at her, I cannot shout.

Only time will tell whether we will be together,
If she believes in me hereafter.

15
Joy

Do you know the power of true joy?
It is like a small girl chirping her song in the morning with her sweet voice, oh boy!

Do not underestimate its power,
It is being happy with the little things that matter,
Even though you have a lot on your platter.

It comes from your inner soul which makes you beautiful,
When you see that the things you have are bountiful.

At times like this, your outside beauty and what nature has given you doesn't matter,
So don't let others' judgments make your thoughts scatter.

True joy brightens up whatever it touches,
But beware of those less fortunate with their jealousy and clutches.

But share it and it multiplies, keep it and it dwindles,
Be with your loved one and see how it enkindles.

Have you experienced the power of true joy?

16
Her

Look at her and you will see sunshine,
Never will you see beauty so refined.

She is insecure at times and makes every effort to improve,
What she does not know is that even mountains she can move.

Mysterious she is and yet she says, there is nothing interesting about her,
With her smartness and wit she can certainly be premier.

Though she may be reserved, she is blunt and strong in her opinion,
She is certainly not fake like the other thousand million.

Try to know about her and you only end up talking about yourself,
It is going to take eternity my friend, until you truly know about her thyself.

A deep-seated pain she carries in her heart, I only came to know now,
Yet, for her sadness to spill into you is what she won't allow.

17
Love Devotion

Madly and deeply in your love,
I have seen numerous dreams with a white dove.

By recalling your affectionate deeds, I praise you with all my heart.
How you lure everyone with your generosity and innocence is an art.

Without even saying anything at all, how do you convince people?
To do what is right, without making others seem feeble.

So obsessed and insane you have made me,
It is like to my mind and heart, you have a key.

Chaotic and irrational are people around me,
When they see me drenched in your love till the highest degree!

18
Fire Love

Let your affinity be natural,
As if you are almost always casual.

For enlightening love, you need to have a genuine need for others,
Don't stop the true feelings that your heart ushers.

Let the fire in you be the liberation,
But remember forced wants only creates bad radiation.

Shun flattering and give praise,
Let the crackling fire in you set your love story ablaze.

19
Dangerous Paths

Are you passing by a sleeping Giant?
Remind yourself that you have to step a little lighter.

Cannot reach the water down below?
Bring a rope tied to a bucket or forgo.

Fire all around you?
Wait for it to recede, or your burns you cannot undo.

Is somebody threatening you?
Panic and you will lose control, rebel and bid yourself adieu.

But there are those who proceed with faith and hope.
A kind of knack to see through the smoke.

It is outrageous to court danger.
But there are those who put both their feet in,
And transform the story altogether.

In a crisis like this they concentrate on their most desirable outcome.
Maintaining inner calm is the rule of thumb.

20
Her Memory

Violently beautiful, speeding across the room,
She moves like a ram and crashes into you, boom boom.

But be mindful of your behaviour and hold her in high regard,
Or in the spur of a moment, she will catch you off guard.

You have to admire her thoughts coming at lightning speed,
When you have only started, she has already finished,
guaranteed.

Play mind games with her and you will ignite this raging fire,
Her thoughts cut through you, turning your status quo so
dire.

When a happy and forgiving soul, she taps her feet on the
floor,
A sweet trail she left behind, her memory he will always
adore.

21
Freedom For Her

Freedom eludes her, but I feel it is only her perception,
She indeed did have her days of glory and exemption.

She has been hit hard and is afraid to climb up the mountain again,
What she needs now, is to make a lot of effort to regain.

Forgetting about the past and her limits is the name of the game,
She needs to take the leap of faith now, or else she will forever remain the same.

Blaming situations and people is what only cowards do,
But a coward she is not, she simply needs to start anew.

Low self-esteem is what she practices nowadays,
If she knows what she is worth, surely everyone she can amaze.

I hope to see her run like a unicorn in a field full of colourful flowers,
Running carefree, yet getting praises and rewards as frequent as rain showers.

22
Give In

Why are your words so pricey?
Do you think others are always so dicey?
Beneath your cold and hard breath,
Lie unspoken words so icy.

If only you would open up,
Then good things would be likely.

Why endure? When you have someone ready to be your emotional punching bag?
Please take a chance, there is no red flag.

23
Precious Character

If it is written in stone,
The truth that gives chills to your bone.

Remember even rocks wither away,
There is nothing that will forever stay.

The same as seasons change,
So does beauty age.

But what remains constant is the soul and spirit,
Not only in your body do they inhabit.

So make sure others recognize you not according to your outer appearance and beauty,
But what lies beneath and makes you more precious than a ruby.

24
I Had a Dream

Out we came from an old wooden house,
Which glorified a green mountain top, living as each other's spouse.

You looked at me with your big bright brown eyes and said,
Let's relax today and let our worries be shred.

We sat on the edge of the cliff gazing at the dawning Sun,
Your skin glowed and I was blinded as the light sprung.

I wish I could emblazon you across the sky today,
Appeared a cloud, looking so much like your pretty face,
To touch it I immediately built a stairway.

Then came a blue-winged parrot and said its sweet, sweet opinion,
"Madam, though I have travelled far and wide,
I haven't seen such beauty,
In any of the changing season.
Oh Lord! Thank you for this chance!
For me to take this glance!"

Soon, the mercury rose and we had to make an escape from the cliff,
We went into our wooden house, the mountain top glyph.

25
A Stranger

A warm slow breeze kisses her soft, glowing skin,
Her bangs dance across, making it look like a movie scene.

The trees too do a slow dance with their whistling leaves,
When she moves across the street,
A great sigh I heave.

A soft, white muslin drapes her body,
It is as if you are seeing someone from heaven,
Do you copy?

A soothing trail of music she leaves behind, audible only to you,
Who is she? Does anyone have a clue?

26
Night To Dawn

The essence of her beauty keeps my mind buzzing with thoughts,
While talking to her my ship runs at 100 knots.

With a thousand million thoughts that churn my mind,
I find it hard to sleep and keep my brain confined.

Is it dawn already? The night has passed!
I would not have guessed that time would go so fast.

And yet, I would long for such nights,
Then wait to make up after a fight,
Because for me it is this that keeps any relation tight.

27
The Wanderer

I wander on the path untrodden every night in search of her.
I look at the stars in the hope that they will lead me to her.

A random ladybug insect comes and says "Don't fall asleep today
Because your reality is better than your dreams."

Yet at dawn, I return dissatisfied.

28
Do You Dream?

This is the world of fantasy;
The one which gives you ecstasy.

This is the place where miracles happen;
Where even the hardest of obstacles are flattened.

A place where you have longed to meet who have already gone;
Where you also meet your ideal swan.

Is there anything you thought you could never do?
Dream, and see it come true.

But there those who dream to live,
Who can make their existence outlive.

Inspired by their dreams they look fear in the eye,
They cripple danger and don't let chances fly.

So make your world vivid with possibilities,
Add colour and forget about your disabilities.

Dig deep into your deepest stratum,
What is it that fulfills your sanctum?

Because this is the way you will acquire,
Whatever is your heart's desire.

Do you dream?

29
The Night

The night is inviting,
To have a great conversation you don't always need a topic so exciting.

The silence of the night creates interest,
It keeps us waiting in mystery,
When your companion strikes the next thought as sharp as the taste of citrus.

It is weird how they wake up in the middle of the night for no reason at all,
They do have similar interests all in all.

We hope that his poems will not be so bad,
That they will make her feel sad.

30
Her Personality

Sweet, soft and so supple as a pillow,
Her heart absorbs everything thus not shallow.

From what I know now she is simple yet sophisticated,
Every time I look at her my pupils are dilated.

Understanding, considerate she is the only one out of the other several,
Who don't even make an effort to listen, and are always ready to wrestle.

A rare find I have made and wish to keep her for long,
She is a friend you would want in your life as she makes your heart dance ping pong.

31
Lucid Dreams

I hope you get whatever you wish for,
But you wish for the right things,
Let your wishes be radical and not based on whims.

Seeing yourself in the mansion of success is not the only goal,
Happiness and fulfillment of noble desires is what nourishes the soul.

Your dream world, let this not be the only place where you take the plunge,
Dig until the core and see what you desire is done.

32
Your Wish

How do I tell you that at criticism I am not an expert?
Because I have recently avoided it along with my opponent's thwart.

I am usually used to telling it like it is,
Minus the whipped cream and the sweetener flavour,

Unintentionally too my speech was so bitter,
Perhaps it was difficult to savour.

I am only learning now how to sugarcoat my opponent's fault,
It is only with time that I can learn to give my criticism a halt.

Why would I want to lose the goodwill and enthusiasm of the other person?
Surely you can tell me if I am wrong and having a misconception.

Encouragement and praise have only made people go far and wide,
But finding faults keeps them away from the heavenly glide.

All I want to say is I prefer to give you winning slings,
Tell me, why would I want to clip a fairy's wings?

33
Perfect One

Have you found that person, the perfect one?
Who is smart, witty, intelligent, good looking, wealthy and comparable to none?

Have you found that person, the right one?
Who will always tolerate you without showing you the gun?

So focus on yourself than changing the other,
Then when you are good, you will have choices one over the other.

Chose a stupid one? Are you heading for tragedy?
Choose the sharpest and the flawless one in the world, alas! A bigger tragedy!

Have someone to complement and complete you,
I may be wrong but I suppose there won't be anyone you would be able to pursue.

34
Anticipation

Please don't keep me guessing,
About our video date, I was not fussing.

How much longer do I have to wait?
To see this pristine pretty princess without a bait?

Only I know how much long I have been waiting to talk to you,
I have been eager to receive the flying kiss that never flew.

Now please hurry up and write to me,
Because in anticipation I am drowning in your love sea.

35
Into Your Dreams

Into your dreams I enter with wild abandon,
Like a sky diver gliding through the air, into the field I then land in.

I tame a wild brown horse without a saddle,
Sitting on the tall galloping horse, to look at you my mellow eyes grapple.

Off we go on a ride, zipping through the forest,
With humongous green trees and different animals our eyes are nourished.

You hold me tight, with fists clamped,
With the elegance of a unicorn running free, on the forest floor the horse stamped.

The sweet and refreshing smell of rain then stimulates our senses,
We head off in a cozy cave, and you look at me with your dilated lenses.

Into the night we talk for hours, enjoying the warmth of the fire,
Cuddling together we sleep, each other's love we admire.

36
Shawty

As evening beckons, it is time for a party,
It is quite fun to meet that Shawty.

She says don't talk to me,
Yet we would go on a laughing spree.

In the midst of everyone's chaos I somehow manage to talk to her,
And then she tells me about ladies I dither.

She came into my life like a storm and how!
I am not blessed enough to handle her now.

Help!

37
My Nephew

He is a jewel in the making,
At three years old he has got everybody guessing,

How smart and witty can someone so young be,
Doing acrobatics at the children's gym for him is easy peasy.

The kind of fun he has makes us want to be a child again,
His modus operandi of making his grandparents dance brings him acclaim.

Mommy says "You are naughty!" when he does a bad deed.
However, when mommy tries to force him to eat,
He throws back "You are naughty!" to mommy indeed.

Choosy he is to who he will give a kiss,
You should consider yourself as the luckiest person on the planet,
And not give his love a miss.

Even when on a trip he will never sit or stand still,
To be the soul of the party he certainly will.

A WHACK! He gets from mommy when running around a road of moving cars.
Then in no time his beloved daddy will heal his scars.

Don't be fooled if his antics make you chuckle,
Because when he is grown up, he is sure going to hustle!

If you want to know more, I will write again,
Don't hesitate because there isn't anything to bargain.

38
Mind Games

Does your mind play games with you?
Is it difficult for you to get your task through?

It all starts with the first moment of the day,
Snooze the alarm and you tend to give it away.

When someone points a finger or shouts at you,
Do you respond or react and make a breakthrough?

Does an uncontrollable situation scare you?
Have hope and you will pull through.

Do the words, effort and pain intimidate you?
Cultivate endurance with perseverance and you will make
your own wishes come true.

In the end, if your mind is stuck in a game of circus,
All you have to do is remember your purpose.

39
Jatinder Sir

To the most noble and soft-hearted man I know,
Such patience and empathy he shows.

His way of enduring even the hardest of situations at work,
Is much deserved than those who have a Merc,

An applause he gets from everyone indeed,
Even when he thinks and perform the smallest of deed.

Don't take to heart if he picks on you,
The lesson you learn should stick in your mind like glue.

He is ambitious and yet adores his colleagues like a cow to her calf,
If there are two of you, he will always divide his affection in half.

At times I feel he doesn't deserve what he is going through,
The stories he hides and suffers will never reach you.

40
Geneva Motor Show

To sketch in front of an audience, is tougher than an exam,
One mistake you make, and questions they will slam.

Here I was promoting my design school at one of the best motor shows in the world,
Where my group thesis project stood out, there the school flag unfurled.

I met so many great designers and personalities from places all over,
Test drives I did and sat in cars we only see in a magazine cover.

All this and I didn't even pay a single penny,
Thanks to my school for giving me this opportunity.

9 789393 809001

Printed by Libri Plureos GmbH in Hamburg,
Germany